SEEN™

True Stories of
Marginalized Trailblazers

Edmonia Lewis

Jasmine Walls · Bex Glendining
Kieran Quigley

Published by
BOOM! BOX™

BOOM! BOX

SEEN: EDMONIA LEWIS, September 2020. Published by BOOM! Box, a division of Boom Entertainment, Inc. SEEN: Edmonia Lewis is ™ & © 2020 Boom Entertainment, Inc. All rights reserved. BOOM! Box™ and the BOOM! Box logo are trademarks of Boom Entertainment, Inc., registered in various countries and categories. All characters, events, and institutions depicted herein are fictional. Any similarity between any of the names, characters, persons, events, and/or institutions in this publication to actual names, characters, and persons, whether living or dead, events, and/or institutions is unintended and purely coincidental. BOOM! Box does not read or accept unsolicited submissions of ideas, stories, or artwork.

BOOM! Studios, 5670 Wilshire Boulevard, Suite 400, Los Angeles, CA 90036-5679. Printed in China. First Printing.

ISBN: 978-1-68415-634-4, eISBN: 978-1-64668-046-7

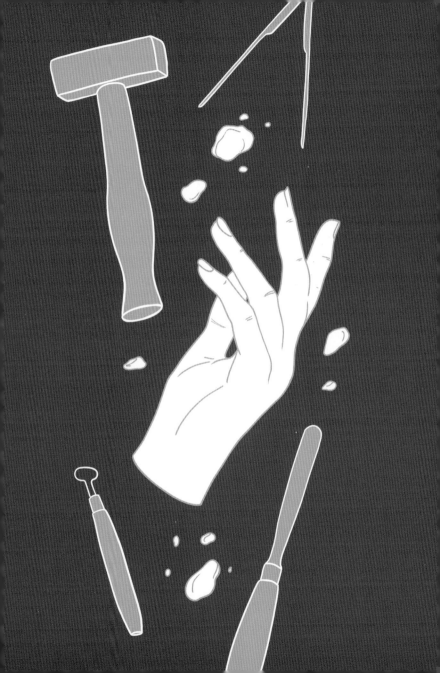

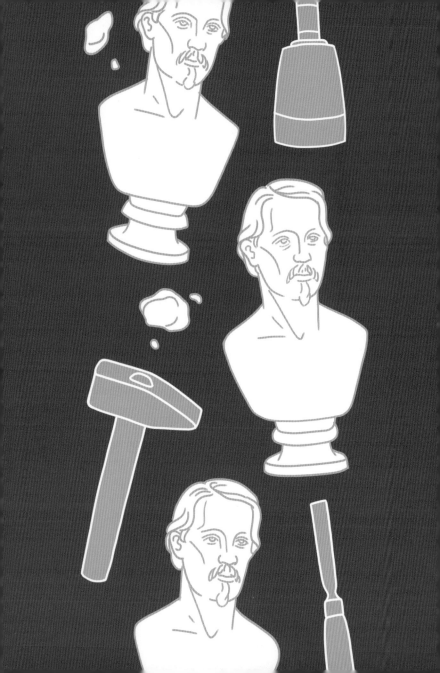

SEEN™

—Edmonia Lewis—

Written by **JASMINE WALLS**

Illustrated by **BEX GLENDINING**

Colored by **KIERAN QUIGLEY**

Lettered by **DC HOPKINS**

Cover by **BEX GLENDINING**

with Colors by **REBECCA NALTY**

Designers **MARIE KRUPINA & SCOTT NEWMAN**

Assistant Editor **KENZIE RZONCA**

Associate Editor **SOPHIE PHILIPS-ROBERTS**

Editor **SHANNON WATTERS**

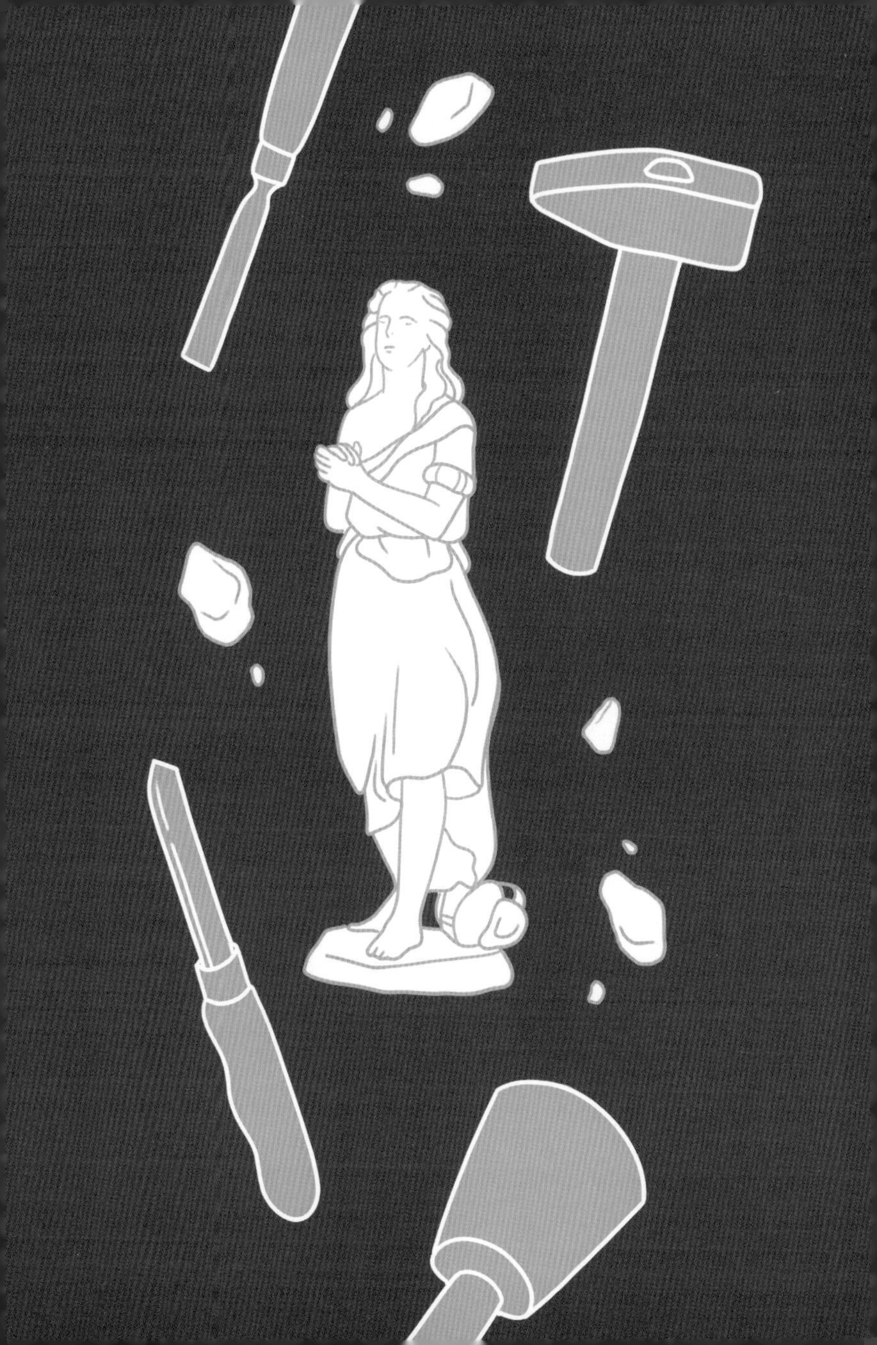

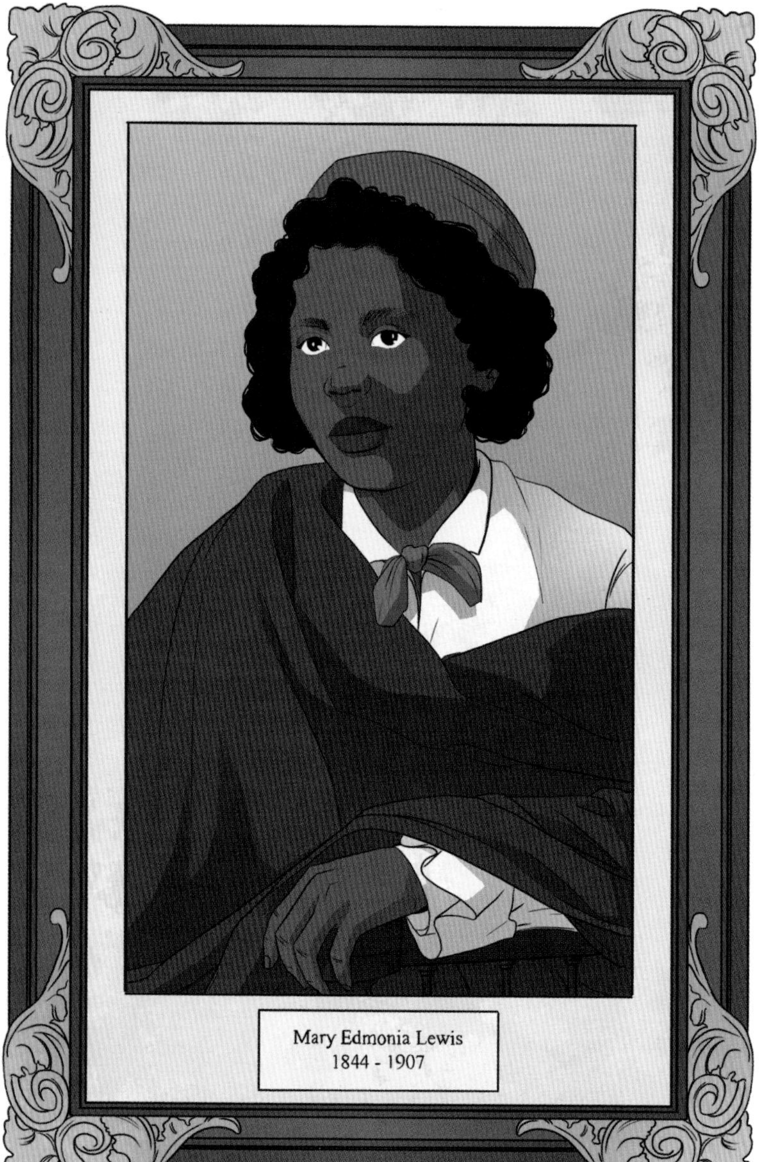
Mary Edmonia Lewis
1844 - 1907

EDMONIA LEWIS WAS MORE THAN JUST A SCULPTOR. NOT ONLY DID SHE HAVE TO NAVIGATE DISPARITIES IN SOCIAL CLASS, WEALTH, LANGUAGE, AND RACIAL EQUALITY, BUT SHE MANAGED TO DO IT SUCCESSFULLY.

SHE WAS A PIONEER, AN INNOVATOR, AND AN INCREDIBLY BRAVE WOMAN WITH A CHEERFUL, BOLD PERSONALITY.

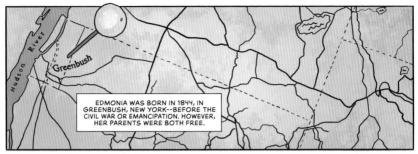

EDMONIA WAS BORN IN 1844, IN GREENBUSH, NEW YORK--BEFORE THE CIVIL WAR OR EMANCIPATION. HOWEVER, HER PARENTS WERE BOTH FREE.

HER MOTHER WAS A MISSISSAUGA OJIBWE WOMAN NAMED CATHERINE MIKE LEWIS.

"MY MOTHER WAS A WILD INDIAN, BORN IN ALBANY, OF COPPER COLOR, AND WITH STRAIGHT, BLACK HAIR. THERE, SHE MADE AND SOLD MOCCASINS."

"MY FATHER, WHO WAS A NEGRO, AND A GENTLEMAN'S SERVANT, SAW HER AND MARRIED HER."

--EDMONIA LEWIS

HER FATHER WAS AN AFRO-HAITIAN MAN WHO WORKED AS A GENTLEMAN'S SERVANT.

HER PARENTS DIED BEFORE SHE TURNED NINE, WHEN SHE AND HER BROTHER SAMUEL WERE TAKEN IN AND RAISED BY HER OJIBWE AUNTS.

SAMUEL BEGAN WORKING AS A BARBER, THE START OF A LONG AND SUCCESSFUL CAREER, WHEN HE WAS JUST TWELVE.

MEANWHILE, EDMONIA STAYED CLOSE TO HER AUNTS, AND GREW UP HELPING THEM SELL THEIR WARES, SUCH AS BASKETS AND MOCCASINS.

AFTER LEAVING HER AUNTS, EDMONIA HAD TO ADJUST TO A WHOLE NEW LIFESTYLE, LANGUAGE, AND WAY OF DRESSING.

EDMONIA WAS KNOWN TO SOMETIMES EXAGGERATE DETAILS OF HER CHILDHOOD WITHIN THE OJIBWE COMMUNITY TO SCANDALIZE PEOPLE WITH STEREOTYPICAL IDEAS ABOUT NATIVE AMERICANS.

IT MUST BE NOTED THOUGH, THAT SHE WAS VERY CLEARLY PROUD OF HER HERITAGE, WHICH SHONE THROUGH NOT ONLY HER WORK, BUT ALSO IN HER OWN WORDS.

"MY FEATURES I TAKE FROM MY FATHER, BUT MY SPIRIT, MY INDUSTRY, AND PERSEVERANCE I GET FROM MY INDIAN MOTHER."

SAMUEL EVENTUALLY HAD TO MOVE WEST TO FIND WORK, THOUGH HE ENCOURAGED EDMONIA TO GO TO SCHOOL AND SENT FUNDS TO CAPTAIN S. R. MILLS, WHO WATCHED OVER HER AS A SORT OF FOSTER PARENT.

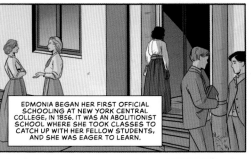

EDMONIA BEGAN HER FIRST OFFICIAL SCHOOLING AT NEW YORK CENTRAL COLLEGE, IN 1856. IT WAS AN ABOLITIONIST SCHOOL WHERE SHE TOOK CLASSES TO CATCH UP WITH HER FELLOW STUDENTS, AND SHE WAS EAGER TO LEARN.

THINGS DIDN'T GO VERY SMOOTHLY, THOUGH, AND IT'S POSSIBLE SHE HAD A HARD TIME SPEAKING ENGLISH. IT'S UNCERTAIN IF HER PROBLEMS WERE DUE TO ENGLISH BEING HER SECOND LANGUAGE, A POSSIBLE SPEECH IMPEDIMENT, OR A CASE OF PEOPLE STEREOTYPING HER IN THEIR WRITING.

I WAS DECLARED TO BE WILD--THEY COULD DO NOTHING WITH ME. OFTEN THEY SAID TO ME, *"HERE IS YOUR BOOK, THE BOOK OF NATURE; COME AND STUDY IT."*

SHE STAYED FOR THREE YEARS BEFORE SHE LEFT THE SCHOOL, POSSIBLY FEELING AS IF THE PROFESSORS HAD GIVEN UP ALL HOPE WITH HER.

DESPITE THIS, EDMONIA CONTINUED HER SCHOOLING AT OBERLIN ACADEMY PREPARATORY SCHOOL, AND FINALLY OBERLIN COLLEGE, THANKS TO FINANCIAL SUPPORT FROM HER BROTHER AND DONATIONS FROM ABOLITIONISTS.

OBERLIN WAS ONE OF THE FIRST HIGHER-LEARNING INSTITUTIONS TO ADMIT PEOPLE OF COLOR, INCLUDING WOMEN, MAKING IT RADICAL FOR THE TIME, BUT IT MUST BE NOTED THAT IT STILL UPHELD AND REINFORCED CERTAIN MINDSETS OF THOSE TIMES AS WELL.

1. BUSINESS
2. LAW & POLITICS
3. HISTORY

THERE WERE CLEAR DISPARITIES BETWEEN THE MEN'S EDUCATION AND THE WOMEN'S...

1. TEACHING
2. SUPPORTING YOUR HUSBAND'S WORK
3. RELIGION

...AS WELL AS BETWEEN WHITE STUDENTS AND STUDENTS OF COLOR.

1. DOMESTIC WORK
2. BEING AN EDUCATED NANNY
3. TAMING YOUR NATURE*

*YEP, IT WAS PRETTY BAD. IT'S 1859, REMEMBER?

EDMONIA WAS ONE OF THIRTY STUDENTS OF COLOR...

...IN A SCHOOL WITH OVER A THOUSAND STUDENTS.

DURING THIS TIME, EDMONIA BOARDED WITH REVEREND JOHN KEEP AND HIS WIFE, WHO WERE OUTSPOKEN SUPPORTERS OF EDUCATION FOR ALL RACES AND GENDERS,

THE TOWN OF OBERLIN ITSELF HAD SEVERAL PROSPEROUS BLACK HOUSEHOLDS WHO OFTEN OFFERED ROOMS FOR BOARDING TO STUDENTS OF THE COLLEGE...

...BUT THERE WERE ALSO MANY WHO OPPOSED THE VIEWS OF THE SCHOOL AND ITS ABOLITIONIST SUPPORTERS.

IT IS DURING THIS TIME OF HER LIFE THAT EDMONIA CHANGED HER NAME TO *MARY EDMONIA LEWIS*, AND IT IS DURING THIS TIME THAT WE FIND THE FIRST RECORD OF HER TAKING ART CLASSES IN A SCHOOL SETTING, THOUGH IT IS CLEAR SHE WAS SKILLED EARLY ON, POSSIBLY DUE TO HER CHILDHOOD ARTISTIC WORK WITH HER AUNTS.

IDEAL AS IT MAY HAVE SOUNDED, OBERLIN WAS FAR FROM PERFECT, AND ALTHOUGH IT WAS THE FIRST COLLEGE THAT INTEGRATED STUDENTS OF DIFFERENT GENDERS AND RACES, EDMONIA STILL SUFFERED FROM CONSTANT RACISM.

SKIN COLOR WASN'T THE ONLY BASIS FOR DISCRIMINATION, EITHER. THE SCHOOL'S AIM WAS TO PREPARE YOUNG WOMEN FOR A LIFE OF TEACHING AND "OTHER DUTIES OF THEIR SPHERE" WHICH OFTEN MEANT DOMESTIC WORK OR AIDING A HUSBAND IN A SMALL BUSINESS.

SHE AND OTHER WOMEN WERE OFTEN OVERLOOKED AND REFUSED PERMISSION TO PARTICIPATE IN CLASSES OR SPEAK PUBLICLY. UNFORTUNATELY, HER COLLEGE DAYS WOULD ONLY GET WORSE.

ANYONE? ANYONE AT ALL?

A SINGLE SCANDAL WOULD DESTROY HER HARD-EARNED REPUTATION.

EDMONIA HAD A GET-TOGETHER WITH HER HOUSEMATES, MARIA MILES AND CHRISTINA ENNES BEFORE A NIGHT OUT.

EXCITED TO SOCIALIZE WITH BOYS WITHOUT A CHAPERONE, EDMONIA SHARED SOME SPICED WINE WITH THE GIRLS DESPITE ALCOHOL BEING BANNED FROM THE HOUSE.

HER CLASSMATES SUDDENLY GOT VERY, VERY SICK.

EDMONIA DID NOT.

THE OFFICIAL DIAGNOSIS WAS THAT THE GIRLS HAS BEEN POISONED, THOUGH NO EVIDENCE WAS PROVIDED. DOCTORS CLAIMED IT WAS "SPANISH FLY", A SUBSTANCE THAT WOULD NOT HAVE BEEN EASY FOR EDMONIA TO PURCHASE.

MARIA AND CHRISTINA CAME CLOSE TO DEATH BEFORE BEGINNING TO RECOVER, BUT THERE WAS NO SOLID PROOF OF FOUL PLAY, SO EDMONIA WAS NOT ARRESTED AT FIRST, AS THE KEEPS DID THEIR BEST TO PROTECT HER.

UNFORTUNATELY, NOTHING COULD SAVE HER LOST FRIENDSHIPS OR RUINED REPUTATION.

ATTEMPTED MURDER AT THE COLLEGE! READ ALL ABOUT IT!

DESPITE ALL EFFORTS OTHERWISE, WORD SPREAD QUICKLY THROUGH THE TOWN OF OBERLIN, WHERE RUMORS AND ACCUSATIONS ONLY GREW--

THIS IS WHAT HAPPENS WHEN WE HAVE *MIXED SCHOOLS!*

IT MUST HAVE BEEN THAT AWFUL GIRL!

ARE THEY PROTECTING MURDERERS NOW? WHERE'S THE JUSTICE?!

--AND THE GENERAL POPULATION WAS QUICK TO POINT OUT EDMONIA AS THE CULPRIT.

VENGEANCE FOR THE GIRLS CAME
ONE NIGHT, WHEN EDMONIA WAS
AMBUSHED, BEATEN, AND ABANDONED
IN AN EMPTY FIELD TO DIE.

MISS LEWIS! CAN YOU HEAR US?!

MISS LEWIS! MARY EDMONIA LEWIS!

A SEARCH WAS SENT OUT WHEN SHE FAILED
TO ARRIVE HOME AND AFTER A LONG NIGHT,
SHE WAS DISCOVERED AND BROUGHT HOME
FOR MEDICAL CARE. SHE WAS PLACED
UNDER ARREST SOON AFTER.

HER TRIAL WAS DELAYED
AFTER EDMONIA MISSED
THE COURT DATE, BECAUSE
SHE WAS TOO INJURED TO
GET OUT OF BED.

THE *CLEVELAND PLAIN DEALER*
DOWNPLAYED HER ATTACK AS A
SIMPLE INCIDENT WHILE SKATING.

...did not come on for trial at the appointed
time, from the fact that the supposed guilty one was ill from the
effects of a severe hurt, received, it is thought, at the hands of
some persons who threw her upon the ice while skating--breaking
a collarbone...

NO EFFORT WAS MADE TO FIND OR PUNISH HER ATTACKERS.

EDMONIA HAD SOME LUCK, IN THAT SHE SECURED HERSELF HELP THROUGH AN OBERLIN ALUMNUS, JOHN MERCER LANGSTON, WHO HAD BEEN OBERLIN'S FIFTH BLACK GRADUATE, AND A SUCCESSFUL LOCAL LAWYER.

HE AGREED TO DEFEND HER DURING THE TRIAL, WHERE SHE HAD TO BE CARRIED INTO THE COURTROOM BY FRIENDS.

HER TRIAL LASTED SIX DAYS.

DESPITE MOST WITNESSES SPEAKING AGAINST HER, LANGSTON CHOSE NOT TO CALL EDMONIA TO THE STAND.

IN THE END, HE GAVE A SIX-HOUR CLOSING ARGUMENT. HE WON THE CASE ON THE ARGUMENT OF *CORPUS DELICTI*, SINCE THE DOCTORS COULD NOT PROVIDE ANY SOLID PROOF OF POISONING.

IN LANGSTON'S AUTOBIOGRAPHY, *FROM THE VIRGINIA PLANTATION TO THE NATIONAL CAPITOL*, HE RECALLED EDMONIA BEING CARRIED OUT OF THE COURTROOM "IN THE ARMS OF HER EXCITED ASSOCIATES AND FELLOW STUDENTS...FULLY VINDICATED IN HER CHARACTER AND NAME."

DESPITE HER PROVEN INNOCENCE, THE FOLLOWING YEAR AT COLLEGE WAS NOT EASY FOR EDMONIA.

IT MUST HAVE BEEN YOU, WHAT WITH YOUR *REPUTATION.*

JUST BEFORE HER LAST TERM, SOMEONE ACCUSED HER OF STEALING ART SUPPLIES. ONCE AGAIN, THERE WAS NO EVIDENCE, BUT THE SCHOOL NO LONGER TRUSTED HER.

EDMONIA HAD NO CHOICE BUT TO DROP OUT WHEN SHE WAS BANNED FROM TAKING THE LAST OF HER CLASSES.

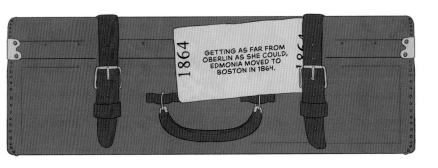

1864

GETTING AS FAR FROM OBERLIN AS SHE COULD, EDMONIA MOVED TO BOSTON IN 1864.

THERE SHE CONNECTED WITH WILLIAM LLOYD GARRISON, AND WAS QUICKLY CONNECTED WITH THE ABOLITIONIST COMMUNITY.

SHE WAS INTERESTED IN SCULPTING, BUT FINDING A TUTOR WAS ANOTHER MATTER. THE FIRST THREE TURNED HER AWAY IMMEDIATELY.

EDMONIA SPENT SEVERAL MONTHS LEARNING BY RECREATING FRAGMENTS OF STATUES BRACKETT GAVE HER.

IT WOULD BE THE ONLY FORMAL TUTELAGE SHE EVER HAD IN SCULPTING.

HERE SHE CRAFTED HER OWN SET OF TOOLS BY HAND, AN IMPORTANT STEP IN HER APPRENTICESHIP.

HER FIRST SCULPTURE SOLD FOR $8, EQUIVALENT TO OVER $120 TODAY.

EDMONIA AND BRACKETT PARTED WAYS SOON AFTER THIS THOUGH, CUTTING TIES IN AUGUST OF 1864, JUST A FEW MONTHS AFTER HE TOOK HER ON AS A STUDENT.

THERE AREN'T ANY DETAILS ON WHY EDMONIA'S TUTELAGE WITH BRACKETT SUDDENLY ENDED, BUT ACCORDING TO A LETTER BY SCULPTOR AND EDMONIA'S CLOSE FRIEND, ANNE WHITNEY, IT DID NOT END WELL.

BRACKETT HAS GIVEN HER UP, AND THEY DID NOT PART WAYS KINDLY.

THIS WILL DO.

IN LATE 1864, EDMONIA OPENED TO THE PUBLIC HER OWN STUDIO-- FUNDED IN LARGE PART BY HER BROTHER--DESPITE ONLY HAVING A FEW MONTHS OF TUTELAGE IN SCULPTING.

HERE SHE HAD SUCCESS SELLING BUSTS OF FAMOUS ABOLITIONISTS OF THE DAY, WHO WERE A POPULAR SUBJECT IN ABOLITIONIST ART COMMUNITIES, AND SEEMED TO BE A PERSONAL INSPIRATION TO HER AS WELL.

ONE OF HER MOST SUCCESSFUL EARLY WORKS WAS A BUST OF COLONEL ROBERT GOULD SHAW, THE COMMANDER OF THE UNION ARMY'S AFRICAN AMERICAN 54TH MASSACHUSETTS INFANTRY REGIMENT DURING THE CIVIL WAR, WHO DIED IN 1863.

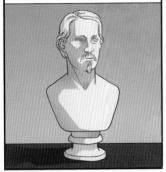

THE LIKENESS IS UNCANNY! HOW MUCH FOR THIS?

THE COLONEL'S FAMILY THEMSELVES BOUGHT THE ORIGINAL BUST.

RECOGNIZING AN OPPORTUNITY, EDMONIA SOLD REPLICAS MADE OF PLASTER THAT WERE MORE AFFORDABLE TO THE PUBLIC.

THEY WERE INCREDIBLY POPULAR, ONE HUNDRED OF THEM SELLING OUT AND SETTING OFF HER CAREER.

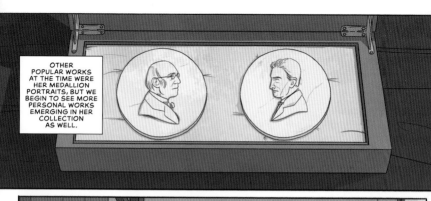

OTHER POPULAR WORKS AT THE TIME WERE HER MEDALLION PORTRAITS, BUT WE BEGIN TO SEE MORE PERSONAL WORKS EMERGING IN HER COLLECTION AS WELL.

THE SONG OF HIAWATHA, A POEM BY HENRY WADSWORTH LONGFELLOW, WAS A COMMON MUSE FOR EDMONIA. POSSIBLY BECAUSE THE POEM WAS INSPIRED BY OJIBWE LEGENDS.

SHE RECREATED WORKS FROM THIS POEM THROUGHOUT HER CAREER, IMPROVING UPON THEM EACH TIME.

EDMONIA BECAME A BIT OF A CELEBRITY WITHIN THE ABOLITIONIST COMMUNITIES, OFTEN WRITTEN ABOUT OR INTERVIEWED BY IMPORTANT WOMEN SUCH AS:

MY NAME IS LYDIA MARIA CHILD, I'M SO PLEASED TO HAVE THIS INTERVIEW WITH YOU.

ELIZABETH PEABODY, FORMERLY FROM *THE DIAL*.

ANNA QUINCY WATERSTON, OF THE *ATLANTIC MONTHLY*.

LAURA BULLARD, FROM THE *LADIES' VISITOR*.

NEWS

Young Sculptress Takes Boston By Storm

THESE ARTICLES CIRCULATED IN IMPORTANT BOSTON AND NEW YORK ABOLITIONIST JOURNALS, LIKE *THE BROKEN FETTER*, THE *CHRISTIAN REGISTER*, AND THE *INDEPENDENT*, AS WELL AS MANY OTHERS.

WHILE EDMONIA APPRECIATED THE POSITIVE RECEPTION IN BOSTON, AND NEVER TURNED AWAY MONETARY AID, SHE HAD NO PATIENCE FOR BEING USED AS A TOOL IN SOMEONE'S HUMANITARIAN ARSENAL IF THEY LACKED REAL INTEREST IN HER ART.

I'VE READ ABOUT YOUR WORK IN THE PAPER, AND HAD TO STOP BY IN PERSON!

THEY DIDN'T DESCRIBE YOUR SCULPTURES MUCH, BUT IT'S SO VERY KIND OF THEM TO SUPPORT A WOMAN LIKE YOURSELF. DEFYING THE ODDS OF YOUR BIRTH, ISN'T THAT JUST MARVELOUS?

SOME PRAISE ME BECAUSE I AM A COLORED GIRL, AND I DON'T WANT THAT KIND OF PRAISE. I HAD RATHER YOU POINT OUT MY DEFECTS, FOR THAT WILL TEACH ME SOMETHING.

SHE WANTED PEOPLE TO APPRECIATE HER WORK, NOT USE HER AS A STEPPING STONE FOR THEIR CAUSES.

I WAS PRACTICALLY DRIVEN TO ROME IN ORDER TO OBTAIN THE OPPORTUNITIES FOR ART CULTURE, AND TO FIND A SOCIAL ATMOSPHERE WHERE I WAS NOT CONSTANTLY REMINDED OF MY COLOR.

THE LAND OF LIBERTY HAD NO ROOM FOR A COLORED SCULPTOR.

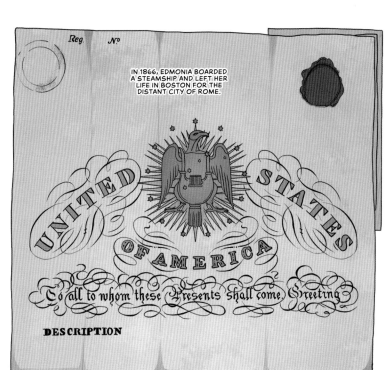

IN 1866, EDMONIA BOARDED A STEAMSHIP AND LEFT HER LIFE IN BOSTON FOR THE DISTANT CITY OF ROME.

UNITED STATES
OF AMERICA

To all to whom these Presents shall come, Greeting

DESCRIPTION

M. Edmonia Lewis is a Black girl sent by subscription to Italy, having displayed great talents as a Sculptor.

Signature of the Bearer

DEPARTMENT OF STATE

ONCE IN ROME, SHE MET HIRAM POWERS, A WELL-KNOWN SCULPTOR WHO INTRODUCED HER TO THE ART COMMUNITY.

WITH HIS HELP, SHE HAD A PLACE TO CREATE AND A FEW CONNECTIONS.

SHE GOT TO KNOW OTHER AMERICAN ARTISTS WHO'D MOVED SO FAR FROM HOME.

IT WASN'T LONG BEFORE SHE HAD A STUDIO OF HER OWN, AND BEGAN MAKING FRIENDS AND MEETING PATRONS.

STARTING A CAREER IN SCULPTING, ESPECIALLY IN MARBLE, IS NOT A CHEAP OR EASY TASK. AT FIRST, EDMONIA HAD TO RELY ON HER PATRONS TO PAY FOR SUPPLIES IN ORDER TO MAKE HER WORK.

ANNE QUINCY WATERSTON'S PATRONAGE FUNDED SOME OF EDMONIA'S FIRST MARBLE PURCHASES IN ROME.

IN ROME, EDMONIA WAS STILL UNDER A FASCINATED SORT OF SCRUTINY, BUT INSTEAD OF BASED SOLELY ON HER SKIN COLOR AND HERITAGE, THAT FOCUS NOW ENCOMPASSED ALL OF HER FELLOW AMERICAN ARTISTS AS WELL.

SHE WAS ABLE TO ENJOY MORE SOCIAL FREEDOM AND BE CLOSER TO THE CENTRAL HUB OF HER FAITH AS A CATHOLIC. IN AN INTERVIEW FROM 1871, SHE STATED:

I HAVE A STRONG SYMPATHY FOR ALL WOMEN WHO HAVE STRUGGLED AND SUFFERED. FOR THIS REASON THE VIRGIN MARY IS VERY DEAR TO ME.

SHE COULD EXPERIMENT MORE WITH HER ART, NO LONGER BOUND BY THE POPULARITY OF ABOLITIONIST POLITICS, AND HAD MORE FREEDOM TO SOCIALIZE AMONG HER PEERS.

IN ORDER TO MAKE HER SCULPTURES, AND TO MAKE A LIVING, EDMONIA NEEDED FUNDS. HER EARLY YEARS IN ROME WERE NOT EASY, AND MONEY WAS A CONSTANT ISSUE.

WITHOUT THE SAFETY NET OF A WEALTHY FAMILY OR REPUTABLE NAME, THIS MEANT A CONSTANT CYCLE OF GAINING PATRONAGE, CREATING WORKS, AND EXPANDING HER NETWORK OF SOCIAL CONNECTIONS.

ALL SO SHE COULD BEGIN THE CYCLE AGAIN.

SOME OF HER PATRONS IN THE US, PARTICULARLY LYDIA MARIA CHILD, WERE CONCERNED THAT EDMONIA WASN'T RESPONSIBLE ENOUGH WITH HER FINANCES. IN ONE LETTER, CHILD CLAIMED THAT IT MUST BE DUE TO HER HERITAGE.

I HAVE OBSERVED THAT SHE HAD NO CALCULATION ABOUT MONEY; WHAT IS RECEIVED WITH FACILITY, IS EXPENDED WITH FACILITY.

THERE WAS SOME TRUTH TO THE MATTER, EDMONIA SPENT A GOOD DEAL OF HER FUNDS ON MUSIC LESSONS...

...ATTENDING SOCIAL GATHERINGS...

...AND LESSONS IN CURRENT POPULAR SPORTS FOR THE GENTEEL LADIES.

TO HER PATRONS, THIS SEEMED AN IMPULSIVE AND IMMATURE WASTE.

MISS LEWIS! AFTER MEETING YOU, I KNEW I HAD TO VISIT AND SEE YOU WORK!

WITH CONTEXT THOUGH, HOW ELSE WAS SHE TO GAIN MORE PATRONAGE? THOSE WITH ENOUGH WEALTH TO BE PATRONS MET ARTISTS IN THESE VERY SAME SOCIAL CIRCLES. EDMONIA WAS BUILDING THE SKILL SETS SHE NEEDED TO BECOME A PART OF THOSE GROUPS.

WHILE IN ROME, IT'S NOT SURPRISING THAT EDMONIA QUICKLY ADOPTED THE NEOCLASSICAL STYLE OF SCULPTURE THAT WAS ALL THE RAGE, RECOGNIZABLE IN THE DEPICTION OF FACES, HAIR, POSES, AND DRAPED, LOOSE CLOTHING.

1871 Bust of Henry Wadsworth Longfellow

NEOCLASSICAL ADJ. *(NĒ-Ō-'KLA-SI-KEL):*

OF, RELATING TO, OR CONSTITUTING A REVIVAL OR ADAPTATION OF THE CLASSICAL ESPECIALLY IN LITERATURE, MUSIC, ART, OR ARCHITECTURE.

MADE IN WHITE MARBLE, OH MY WORD!

IS...IS THAT ALLOWED?

SHE WAS UNIQUE AMONG HER PEERS FOR FOCUSING ON BLACK AND NATIVE AMERICAN SUBJECTS DEPICTED IN MARBLE, SUCH AS *FOREVER FREE* AND HER MANY ITERATIONS OF THE CHARACTERS FROM *THE SONG OF HIAWATHA*.

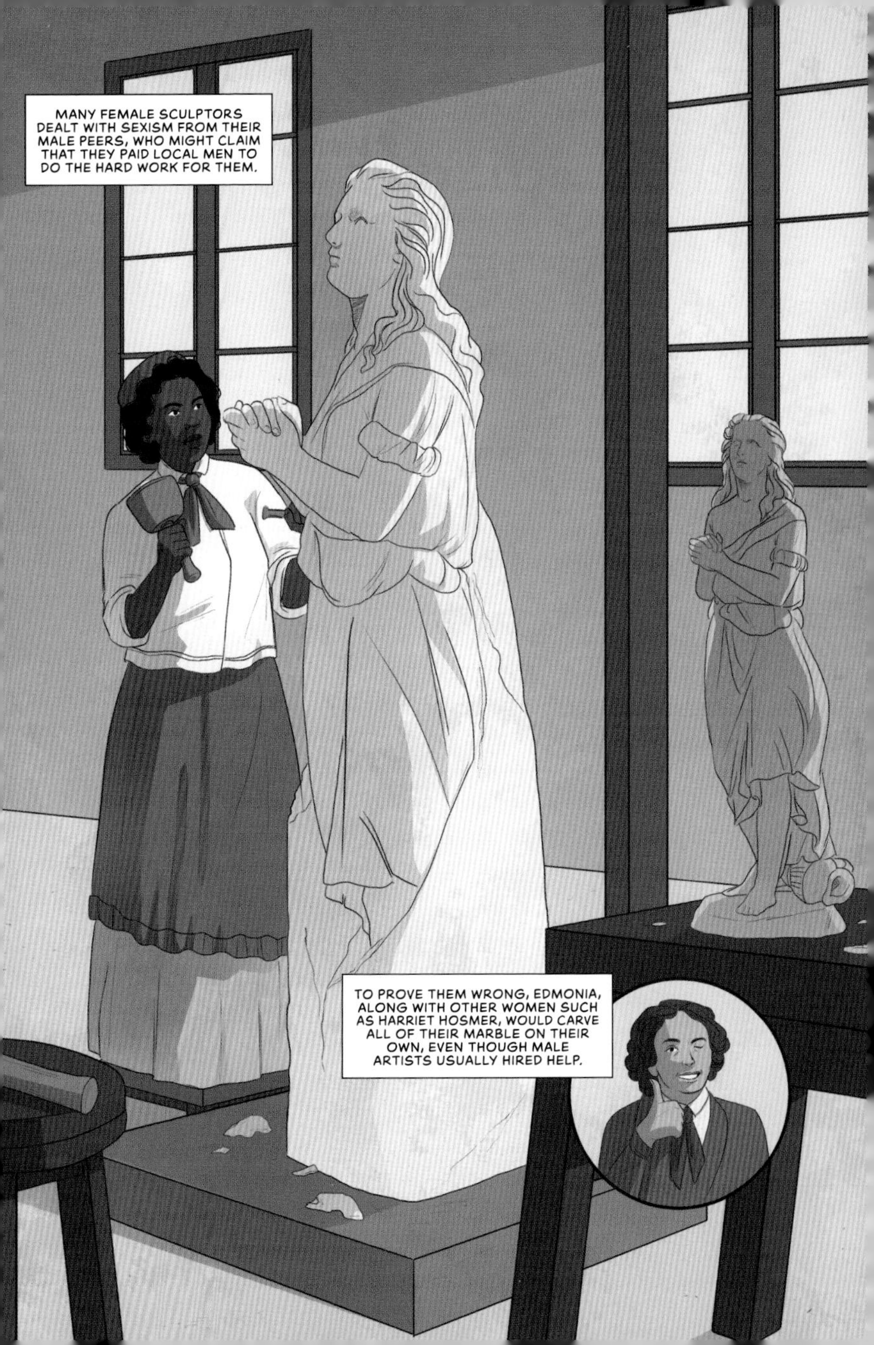
MANY FEMALE SCULPTORS DEALT WITH SEXISM FROM THEIR MALE PEERS, WHO MIGHT CLAIM THAT THEY PAID LOCAL MEN TO DO THE HARD WORK FOR THEM.
TO PROVE THEM WRONG, EDMONIA, ALONG WITH OTHER WOMEN SUCH AS HARRIET HOSMER, WOULD CARVE ALL OF THEIR MARBLE ON THEIR OWN, EVEN THOUGH MALE ARTISTS USUALLY HIRED HELP.

IT WASN'T THE ONLY TACTIC SHE USED; EDMONIA WAS A
SHREWD AND CLEVER WOMAN WHO DIDN'T SHY AWAY FROM
USING UNORTHODOX METHODS, AND HER APPROACH TO
GAINING PATRONAGE AND CLIENTELE WAS NO DIFFERENT.

PERHAPS A
FLATTERING FAMILY
BUST? A BELOVED
HERO?

SHE WOULD SURPRISE
PATRONS OR SOCIAL
CLUBS WITH A
FINISHED SCULPTURE,
AND THEN ASK FOR
THEM TO PAY FOR IT.

YOUR
DELIVERY FROM
ROME, SIR.

*WHAT
DELIVERY?*

IT WAS PERHAPS NOT THE BEST
APPROACH, AND MAY HAVE DAMAGED
SOME RELATIONSHIPS WITH HER
PATRONS, BUT NO ONE COULD SAY
IT WASN'T A MEMORABLE AND
FAIRLY EFFECTIVE METHOD.

IT IS IMPORTANT TO REMEMBER THAT EDMONIA HAD NO FAMILY CONTACTS TO RELY ON, AND NO INCOME BEYOND THE FUNDING OF HER PATRONS, HER SALES, AND THE HELP HER BROTHER COULD AFFORD TO SEND TO HER.

THANK GOODNESS MY FATHER IS FRIENDS WITH DOCTORS, THE MATERIAL THEY'VE SHARED HAS BEEN SO HELPFUL.

ILLUSTRATIONS ARE ONLY SO HELPFUL. I'VE ARRANGED FOR PRIVATE TUTORING.

CAN YOU IMAGINE HAVING TO GO TO A *PUBLIC LECTURE WITH MEN?*

SHE HAD LITTLE ACCESS TO THE UPPER CLASS ELITE THAT MANY OF HER PEERS WERE CONNECTED WITH.

ANY STUDIES SHE MIGHT TAKE TO IMPROVE HER ART WERE HELD BACK BY A STRICT DIVIDE OF GENDER. WOMEN WERE BARRED FROM ATTENDING MEDICAL ANATOMY SESSIONS, WHICH MANY ARTISTS AND SCULPTORS USED TO IMPROVE THE ACCURACY OF THEIR FIGURES.

THE WOMEN WHO DID ATTEND THE LECTURES WERE USUALLY SHAMED AND BULLIED OUT OF THEM. THOMAS CRAWFORD WROTE VICIOUSLY ABOUT FELLOW SCULPTOR HARRIET HOSMER, WHO CLEARLY REFUSED TO BE COWED.

"MISS HOSMER'S WANT OF MODESTY IS ENOUGH TO DISGUST A DOG. SHE HAS HAD CASTS FOR THE ENTIRE MODEL MADE AND EXHIBITED THEM IN A SHOCKING INDECENT MANNER TO ALL THE YOUNG ARTISTS WHO CALL UPON HER. THIS IS GOING IT RATHER STRONG."

ONE OF HER SUPPORTERS, LYDIA MARIA CHILD, WHO STAYED IN CONTACT WITH EDMONIA FOR YEARS, TOOK TO ATTEMPTING SOME ADVICE EARLY ON.

SHE ENCOURAGED EDMONIA TO START ON A SMALLER SCALE AND DO MASONRY WORK TO DEVELOP HER SKILLS BEFORE ATTEMPTING LARGER SCULPTURES THAT MIGHT BE BEYOND HER SKILL SET.

EDMONIA HAD NO INTEREST IN THAT PATH AND FORGED FORTH ANYWAY, TO MIXED RESULTS.

EDMONIA'S LACK OF IN-DEPTH TUTELAGE SHOWED ON HER LARGER FULL-BODY WORKS. ART CRITICS POINTED OUT ISSUES WITH ANATOMY, ESPECIALLY IN HER EARLIER WORKS, SUCH AS *FOREVER FREE*--WHICH LYDIA MARIA CHILD REFUSED TO SUPPORT--AND LATER, AN ILL-FATED ATTEMPT AT REPLICATING MICHELANGELO'S WORK, SOMETHING MANY SCULPTORS DID AS A SHOW OF PRACTICE AND SKILL.

HARDLY GRACEFUL, IS IT?

OH DEAR, WHAT A WASTE OF FINE MARBLE!

PERHAPS SHE'S ONLY SEEN THE ORIGINAL FROM FAR AWAY?

SHE AND LYDIA MARIA CHILD EVENTUALLY CUT TIES, AND IN LETTERS TO FRIENDS, CHILD EXPRESSED HER FRUSTRATION WITH EDMONIA'S STUBBORNNESS, AND LATER, THEIR INABILITY TO RECONCILE.

WHAT SHE UNDERTAKES TO DO...SHE WILL DO, THOUGH SHE HAS TO CUT THROUGH THE HEART OF A MOUNTAIN WITH A PEN KNIFE.

THERE IS AT PRESENT A LITTLE COOLNESS BETWEEN US.

EDMONIA CLEARLY LEARNED AS SHE WORKED, IMPROVING UPON HER ART WITH EACH NEW PIECE, AND IT SHOWS IN HER LATER SURVIVING SCULPTURES.

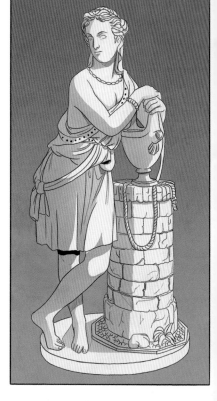

HER MOST FAMOUS, AND ARGUABLY HER MOST IMPRESSIVE SCULPTURE, WAS REVEALED TO THE PUBLIC IN 1876, AT THE CENTENNIAL EXPOSITION IN PHILADELPHIA. AN ASTOUNDING 3,015 POUND SOLID MARBLE SCULPTURE DEPICTING, AND APTLY NAMED, *THE DEATH OF CLEOPATRA.*

THE SCULPTURE TOOK HER FOUR YEARS TO MAKE, AND SEVERAL TRIPS ACROSS THE OCEAN FOR EXHIBITIONS TO FUND THE EFFORT.

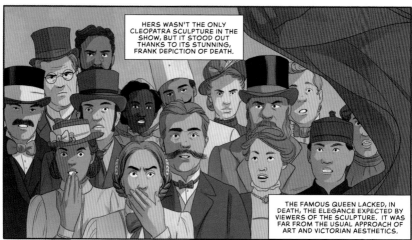

HERS WASN'T THE ONLY CLEOPATRA SCULPTURE IN THE SHOW, BUT IT STOOD OUT THANKS TO ITS STUNNING, FRANK DEPICTION OF DEATH.

THE FAMOUS QUEEN LACKED, IN DEATH, THE ELEGANCE EXPECTED BY VIEWERS OF THE SCULPTURE. IT WAS FAR FROM THE USUAL APPROACH OF ART AND VICTORIAN AESTHETICS.

IT'S CERTAINLY A BOLD CHOICE.

IT'S AN INSULT TO THE ART FORM!

I CAN'T TELL IF I LIKE IT OR NOT...

WHAT A SIGHT!

IT DREW SOME NEGATIVE OPINIONS, BUT ALSO MUCH ACCLAIM AND THOUSANDS OF VIEWERS CAME TO SEE IT. J.S. INGRAHAM WROTE THAT IT WAS *"THE MOST REMARKABLE PIECE OF SCULPTURE IN THE AMERICAN SECTION."*

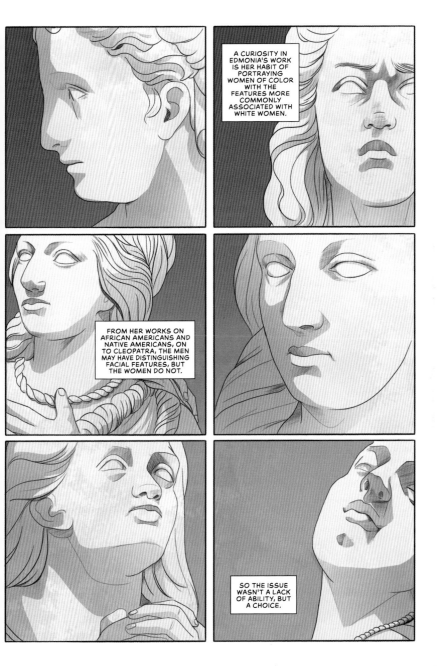

A CURIOSITY IN EDMONIA'S WORK IS HER HABIT OF PORTRAYING WOMEN OF COLOR WITH THE FEATURES MORE COMMONLY ASSOCIATED WITH WHITE WOMEN.

FROM HER WORKS ON AFRICAN AMERICANS AND NATIVE AMERICANS, ON TO CLEOPATRA, THE MEN MAY HAVE DISTINGUISHING FACIAL FEATURES, BUT THE WOMEN DO NOT.

SO THE ISSUE WASN'T A LACK OF ABILITY, BUT A CHOICE.

EDMONIA WAS CLEAR THAT SHE HAD NO DESIRE TO BE JUDGED BY HER SKIN COLOR BEFORE HER ART.

CONSIDERING THE TIME PERIOD, IT IS VERY LIKELY THAT HAD SHE NOT DONE SO, ANY WOMAN OF COLOR IN HER SCULPTURES MIGHT HAVE BEEN SEEN AS A SORT OF SELF PORTRAIT AND ANY CRITICISM OF IT WOULD ALSO BE TURNED ON HER.

BUT *THE DEATH OF CLEOPATRA* ALSO STANDS OUT AMONG HER WORKS FOR MORE SURPRISING REASONS.

AFTER THE EXPOSITION, EDMONIA CHOSE TO KEEP IT IN STORAGE RATHER THAN BEAR THE COSTS OF SHIPPING IT BACK TO ROME WHEN IT FAILED TO SELL. THEN, FOR NEARLY A CENTURY, IT SEEMED TO VANISH.

WE NOW KNOW THE STORY, THANKS TO THE EFFORTS OF PEOPLE WHO WORKED DILIGENTLY TO KEEP EDMONIA AND HER LEGACY FROM VANISHING INTO THE DEPTHS OF HISTORY. BUT BEFORE THEN, *THE DEATH OF CLEOPATRA* SEEMED TO HAVE SIMPLY WALKED OFF, TAKING HER MARBLE THRONE WITH HER.

THE TRUE STORY IS ALMOST AS STRANGE.

IT'S PERFECT! WE'LL LOOK LIKE THE CLASSIEST BAR IN TOWN!

SOMEHOW, *THE DEATH OF CLEOPATRA* ENDED UP IN A BAR AFTER IT WAS DISPLAYED, BUT DIDN'T SELL, AT THE CHICAGO INTERSTATE EXPOSITION IN 1878.

I FEEL LIKE I'M BEING WATCHED WITH THAT THING IN HERE.

REALLY? I LIKE IT. BIT OUT OF PLACE THOUGH.

NOW THAT YOU MENTION IT, THAT'S A STATUE OF CLEOPATRA, RIGHT?

"BLIND JOHN" CONDON, WHO OWNED A RACETRACK IN A NEARBY NEIGHBORHOOD, BOUGHT *THE DEATH OF CLEOPATRA* TO PLACE WHERE HIS BELOVED RACEHORSE OF THE SAME NAME WAS BURIED, RIGHT IN FRONT OF THE TRACK.

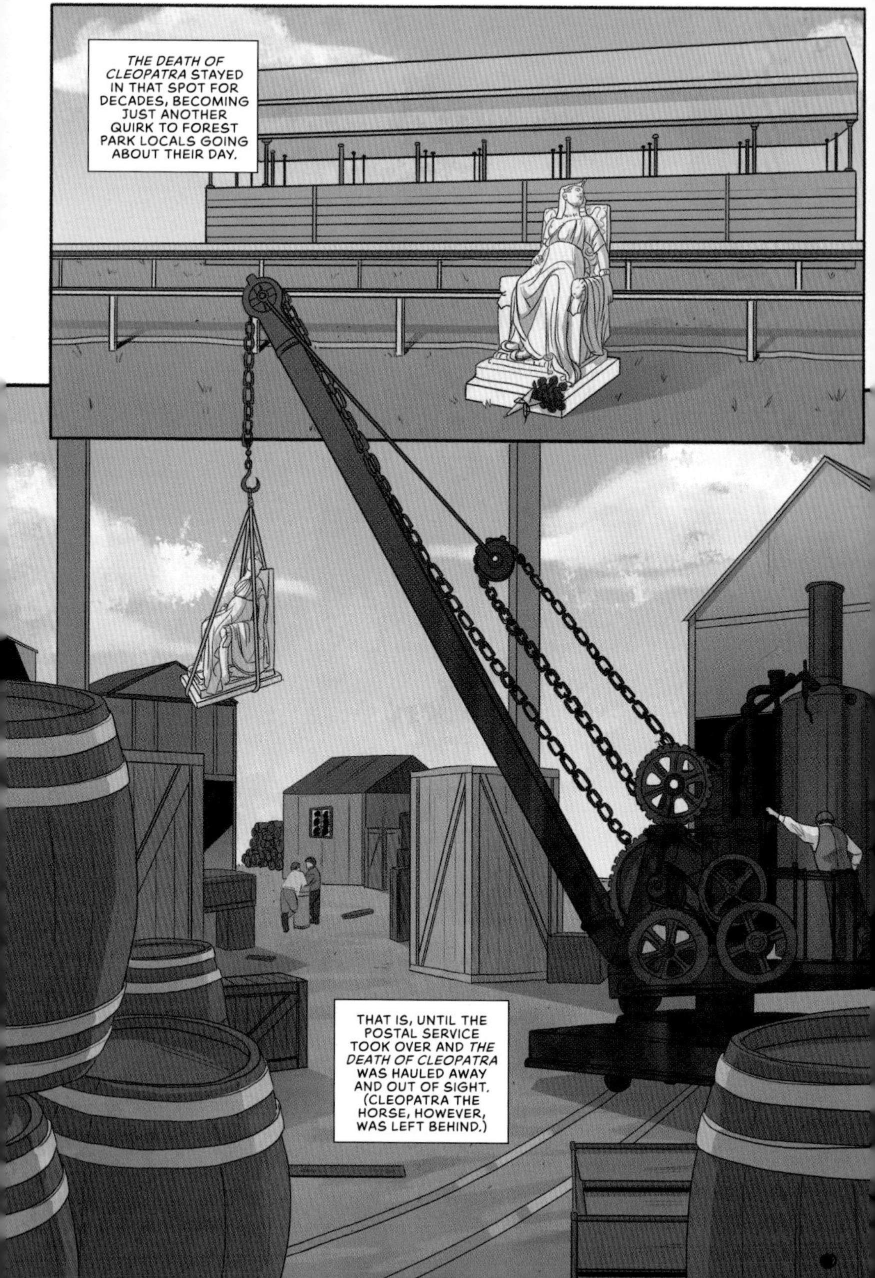
THE DEATH OF CLEOPATRA STAYED IN THAT SPOT FOR DECADES, BECOMING JUST ANOTHER QUIRK TO FOREST PARK LOCALS GOING ABOUT THEIR DAY.
THAT IS, UNTIL THE POSTAL SERVICE TOOK OVER AND THE DEATH OF CLEOPATRA WAS HAULED AWAY AND OUT OF SIGHT. (CLEOPATRA THE HORSE, HOWEVER, WAS LEFT BEHIND.)

IT WAS IN THIS CONSTRUCTION STORAGE THAT MORE DAMAGE WAS DONE TO THE STATUE THAN TIME, WEATHER, AND CARELESS BARKEEPS COULD MANAGE.

A BOY SCOUT TROOP, EAGER FOR BADGES, TOOK IT UPON THEMSELVES TO "RESTORE" *THE DEATH OF CLEOPATRA*, INCLUDING A FRESH NEW PAINT JOB.

LUCKILY, A HERO ARRIVED IN THE FORM OF DR. JAMES ORLAND, WHO HAD THE STATUE PLACED IN HIS POSSESSION AND MOVED TO A PRIVATE STORAGE FACILITY, SAFE FROM THE HANDS OF WELL-MEANING BUT DESTRUCTIVE "REPAIRS."

AS PART OF THE FOREST PARK HISTORICAL SOCIETY, DR. ORLAND CONTACTED THE METROPOLITAN MUSEUM OF ART ABOUT THE STATUE, BUT HAD FEW ANSWERS...

...ON THE EAST COAST, AN ASSISTANT PROFESSOR AT MIT NAMED MARILYN RICHARDSON WAS WORKING ON A BIOGRAPHY OF EDMONIA LEWIS, AND WAS TRYING TO SOLVE THE MYSTERY OF THE LOST *CLEOPATRA.*

*TODAY, SHE'S AN AFRICAN AMERICAN ART SCHOLAR AND MUSEUM CURATOR!

YOU DON'T JUST *LOSE* A 3,000 POUND STATUE.

HER SEARCH EVENTUALLY CROSSED PATHS WITH THE FOREST PARK HISTORICAL SOCIETY, WHO HAD A FAMILIAR-SOUNDING SCULPTURE TUCKED AWAY IN A STORAGE FACILITY. SHE VERIFIED THAT IT MIGHT JUST BE THE *CLEOPATRA* SHE WAS LOOKING FOR, BUT HER WORK DIDN'T STOP THERE.

THE NEXT STEP WAS A CALL TO DOROTHY PORTER WESLEY, AN AFRICAN AMERICAN BIBLIOGRAPHER, WHO WORKED WITH HER TO CONTACT THE SMITHSONIAN AMERICAN ART MUSEUM.

THE CURATOR AT THE TIME, GEORGE GURNEY, CONFIRMED THE SCULPTURE'S LEGITIMACY. IT HAD OUTLASTED THE RACETRACK, GOLF COURSE, AND A WORLD WAR II MUNITIONS FACTORY, BEFORE IT WAS RELOCATED.

FINALLY, IN 1994, THE FOREST PARK HISTORICAL SOCIETY DONATED *THE DEATH OF CLEOPATRA* TO HER NEW HOME AT THE SMITHSONIAN AMERICAN ART MUSEUM.

CHICAGO ARTIST AND RESTORATION EXPERT, DR. ANDREZEJ DAJNOWSKI TEAMED UP WITH THE SMITHSONIAN TO PROPERLY RESTORE *THE DEATH OF CLEOPATRA* TO HER FORMER GLORY, WHICH WAS NO EASY TASK.

FIRST THE PAINT HAD TO BE STRIPPED AWAY. THEN THE NOSE, SANDALS, HANDS, AND CHIN NEEDED TO BE REPAIRED, DUE TO SUGARING DAMAGE FROM EXPOSURE TO THE ELEMENTS. ALL AT A TOTAL COST OF AROUND $30,000.

MY WORK HERE IS DONE.

THIS VERY SCULPTURE NOW HAS A HOME AT THE SMITHSONIAN AMERICAN ART MUSEUM.

BEFORE THE MARBLE *CLEOPATRA* HAD A CHANCE TO BE FORGOTTEN, EDMONIA HAD RETURNED TO ROME AND WAS AT THE HEIGHT OF HER RENOWN.

EVEN FORMER PRESIDENT ULYSSES S. GRANT MODELED IN PERSON TO GET A PORTRAIT MADE BY HER IN 1877, A SURE BOOST TO HER REPUTATION.

HER ABILITY TO CAPTURE LIKENESS IN FACES WAS SOMETHING SHE'D SHOWN A TALENT FOR SINCE THE BEGINNING OF HER CAREER, AND IT CONTINUED IN HER FAVOR.

WITH THE DEMAND FOR NEOCLASSICAL STYLE FALLING AFTER THE 1880S, EDMONIA BEGAN TO STRUGGLE FINDING PATRONS AND BUYERS TO INVEST IN HER ART.

THEY'RE VERY NICE, BUT IT'S NOT 1870 ANYMORE. OUR GUESTS WILL THINK WE'RE *OLD-FASHIONED.*

WOULD YOU CONSIDER SCULPTING CHERUBS, MISS LEWIS?

WELL, I SUPPOSE I COULD!

SHE DIDN'T LET THAT STOP HER THOUGH, AND THE ROMAN CATHOLIC CHURCH WOULD BECOME A MAJOR SOURCE OF INCOME FOR HER.

SHE STILL MADE PORTRAIT BUSTS, PROVEN BY THE SCULPTURE OF CHARLES SUMNER SHE MADE FOR THE 1895 ATLANTA EXPOSITION.

BUT DEMAND WAS IN DECLINE, AND EDMONIA'S ART WAS SLOWLY SHADOWED BY THE NEWER TRENDS OF THE ART WORLD.

THE PERSONAL DETAILS OF EDMONIA'S LATER YEARS ARE MOSTLY UNKNOWN, BUT HER BROTHER, SAMUEL, HAD A SUCCESSFUL CAREER AS A BARBER, LATER MOVING ONTO INVESTING IN COMMERCIAL REAL ESTATE.

HE MET A WIDOW, MELISSA RAILEY BRUCE, WHOM HE MARRIED IN 1884. SHE HAD SIX CHILDREN FROM HER PREVIOUS MARRIAGE, AND LATER THE TWO OF THEM HAD A SON, WHO THEY NAMED AFTER SAMUEL.

SAMUEL DIED IN 1896, BUT DESPITE HOW DIFFERENT THEIR LIVES WERE, SAMUEL AND EDMONIA STAYED IN TOUCH THROUGH LETTERS, AND HE SUPPORTED HER CAREER FROM THE START.

EDMONIA LEWIS WAS A SOCIAL GLOBE-TROTTER, WITH PASSPORTS STAMPED FROM ALL OVER. NOT MUCH OTHER THAN HER TRAVELS ARE KNOWN ABOUT HER LATER LIFE THOUGH, AND SHE NEVER CHOSE TO MARRY.

SHE WAS KNOWN FOR BEING CHEERFUL, ENERGETIC--MAYBE EVEN A LITTLE TOO ENTHUSIASTIC SOMETIMES--AND A HARD WORKER. SHE WORKED AND LIVED IN ROME UNTIL 1901, WHEN SHE MADE HER FINAL MOVE TO LONDON.

FREDRICK DOUGLASS, TRAVELLING WITH HIS WIFE, HELEN, ONCE MET WITH EDMONIA IN ROME AND, IMPRESSED WITH HER FAMILIARITY WITH THE CITY AND HER CAREER, DESCRIBED HER AS:

VERY CHEERFUL AND HAPPY AND SUCCESSFUL. SHE MAKES US OBLIGED TO HER FOR KINDLY OFFERING TO HELP US IN ANY WAY SHE COULD AND SHE CERTAINLY SEEMS ABLE TO SERVE US IN MANY WAYS.

TO COMMEMORATE THE OCCASION, EDMONIA SCULPTED A BUST OF FREDRICK DOUGLASS SOON AFTER, AND HE CLAIMED THAT HER ITALIAN WAS EXCEPTIONAL, DESPITE ANY ISSUES SHE MAY HAVE HAD WITH ENGLISH.

EDMONIA SPENT THE LATER YEARS OF HER LIFE IN LONDON, ENGLAND, SPECIFICALLY IN THE HAMMERSMITH AREA, WHERE SHE DIED OF BRIGHT'S DISEASE ON SEPTEMBER 17, 1907.

SHE IS BURIED IN ST. MARY'S ROMAN CATHOLIC CEMETERY IN LONDON, WITH HER GRAVE NOW RESTORED AFTER A SUCCESSFUL CROWDFUNDING CAMPAIGN RUN BY BOBBIE RENO, AN EAST GREENBUSH TOWN HISTORIAN, IN 2017.

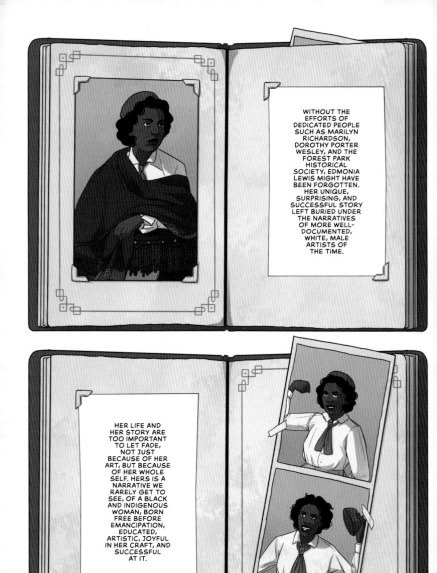

WITHOUT THE EFFORTS OF DEDICATED PEOPLE SUCH AS MARILYN RICHARDSON, DOROTHY PORTER WESLEY, AND THE FOREST PARK HISTORICAL SOCIETY, EDMONIA LEWIS MIGHT HAVE BEEN FORGOTTEN. HER UNIQUE, SURPRISING, AND SUCCESSFUL STORY LEFT BURIED UNDER THE NARRATIVES OF MORE WELL-DOCUMENTED, WHITE, MALE ARTISTS OF THE TIME.

HER LIFE AND HER STORY ARE TOO IMPORTANT TO LET FADE, NOT JUST BECAUSE OF HER ART, BUT BECAUSE OF HER WHOLE SELF. HERS IS A NARRATIVE WE RARELY GET TO SEE, OF A BLACK AND INDIGENOUS WOMAN, BORN FREE BEFORE EMANCIPATION, EDUCATED, ARTISTIC, JOYFUL IN HER CRAFT, AND SUCCESSFUL AT IT.

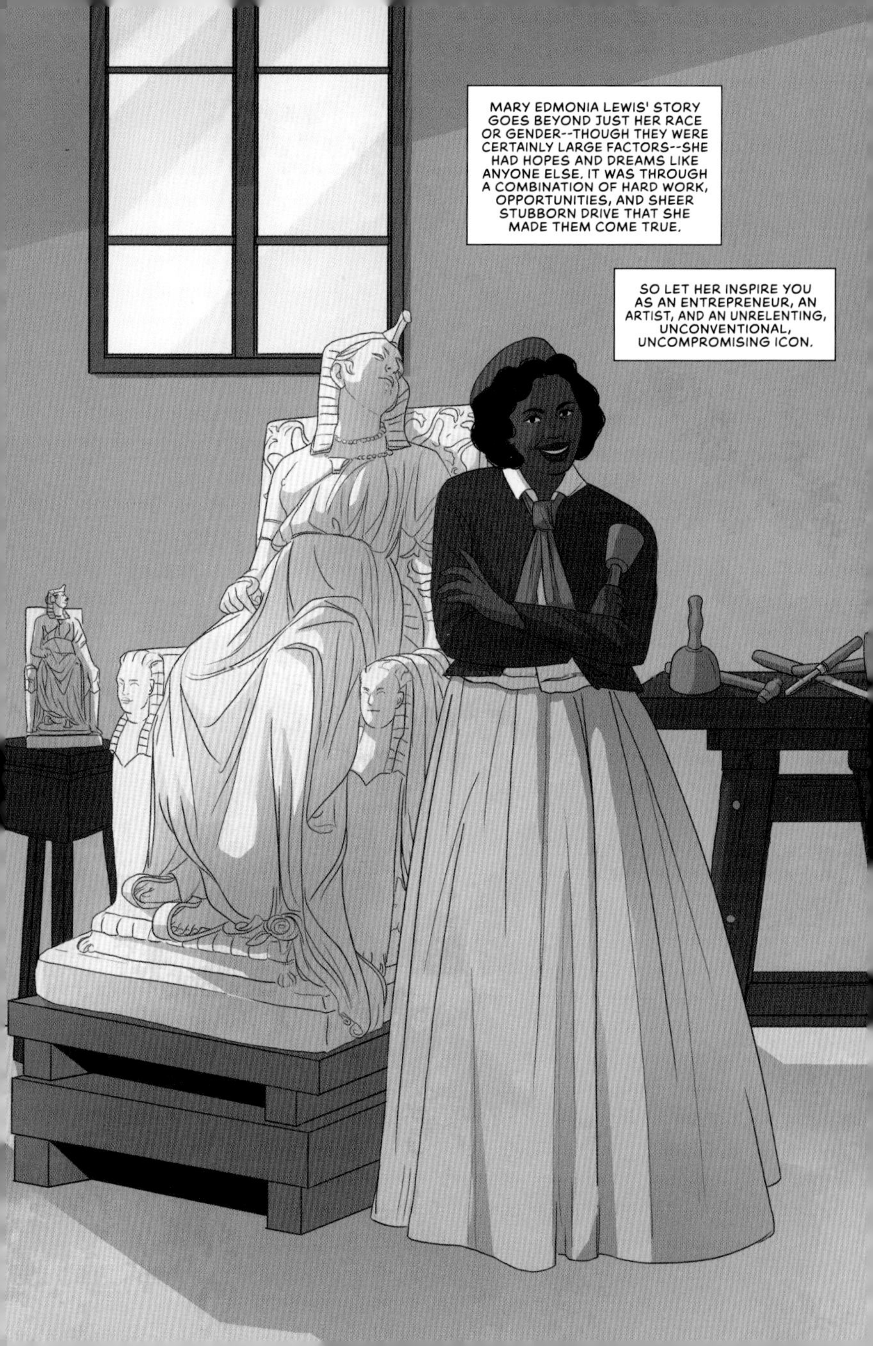
MARY EDMONIA LEWIS' STORY GOES BEYOND JUST HER RACE OR GENDER--THOUGH THEY WERE CERTAINLY LARGE FACTORS--SHE HAD HOPES AND DREAMS LIKE ANYONE ELSE. IT WAS THROUGH A COMBINATION OF HARD WORK, OPPORTUNITIES, AND SHEER STUBBORN DRIVE THAT SHE MADE THEM COME TRUE.
SO LET HER INSPIRE YOU AS AN ENTREPRENEUR, AN ARTIST, AND AN UNRELENTING, UNCONVENTIONAL, UNCOMPROMISING ICON.

Extra Notes

IT SHOULD BE NOTED THAT EDMONIA'S MOTHER WAS NOT *TECHNICALLY* A "FULL-BLOODED" NATIVE WOMAN, THOUGH THE CONTEXT OF EDMONIA'S QUOTE AND THE INTENT OF HER MEANING CAN'T FULLY BE KNOWN. HER MOTHER, CATHERINE LEWIS, WAS OF MIXED HERITAGE. BORN IN CANADA, SHE SPENT HER YOUNGER YEARS ON THE CREDIT RIVER RESERVE, WHERE EDMONIA'S GRANDMOTHER WAS FROM.

EDMONIA'S MATERNAL GRANDFATHER, JOHN MIKE, WAS A BLACK MAN WHO ESCAPED SLAVERY. DUE TO MEMBERSHIP WITHIN THE RESERVATION BEING DERIVED FROM FATHERS, THE ELDERS MOVED TO DENY ENTITLEMENT TO GOVERNMENT GRANTS TO CATHERINE, HER FATHER, AND HER SISTERS. THOUGH THEY HAD NO LEGAL POWER TO DO SO, IT PUT PRESSURE ON THE FAMILY AND THEY ENDED UP MOVING SEVERAL TIMES BEFORE EVENTUALLY SETTLING IN THE TOWN KNOWN AS GREENBUSH, WHERE EDMONIA WAS BORN.

EDMONIA'S STUDIO IN ROME HAD PREVIOUSLY BELONGED TO ANTONIO CANOVA, AN 18TH CENTURY SCULPTOR. THE EARLY DAYS OF HER CAREER IN ROME WERE MAINLY FUNDED BY BOSTON ABOLITIONIST PATRONS, AS WELL AS SOME NEW INTERNATIONAL PATRONS WHO WERE IMPRESSED BY HER WORK, SUCH AS CHARLOTTE CUSHMAN, LYDIA MARIA CHILD, AND MARIA WESTON CHAPMAN.

Sources Consulted in the Writing & Drawing of this Graphic Novel:

1. Buick, Kirsten Pai. *Child of the Fire: Mary Edmonia Lewis and the Problem of Art History's Black and Indian Subject.* Duke University Press, 2010.

2. *Edmonia Lewis*, www.edmonialewis.com/.

3. Henderson, Albert. Henderson, Harry. *The Indomitable Spirit of Edmonia Lewis, A Narrative Biography.* Esquiline Hill Press, 2012.

4. Nelson, Charmaine A. *The Color of Stone: Sculpting the Black Female Subject in Nineteenth-Century America.* University of Minnesota Press, 2007.

5. Smithsonian Institution Archives. *Edmonia Lewis.* https://americanart.si.edu/artist/edmonia-lewis-2914.

6. Wolfe, Rinna Evelyn. *Edmonia Lewis: Wildfire in Marble.* Dillon Press, 1998.

7. Wikipedia contributors. "Edmonia Lewis." *Wikipedia, The Free Encyclopedia.* Wikipedia, The Free Encyclopedia, 9 Mar. 2020. Web. 15 Apr. 2020.

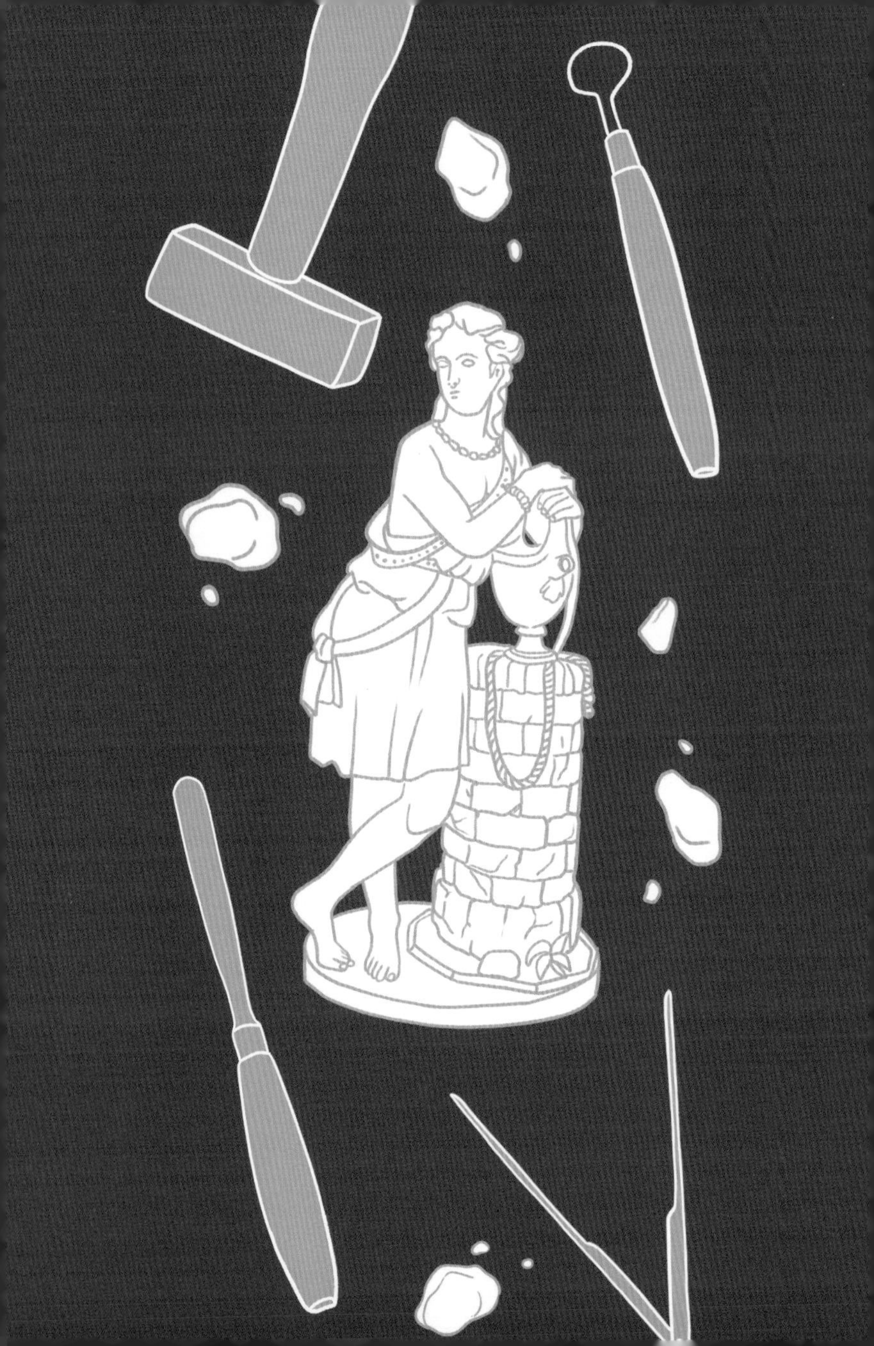

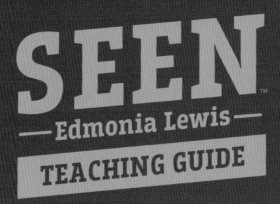

Learning Standards

The questions and activities in this teacher guide correlate with the following Common Core English Language Arts Standards (www.corestandards.org) for Grades 6, 7-10, and 9-10:

ELA Reading: Literature Standards
- Key Ideas and Details RL.6-10.1, RL.6-10.2, RL.6-10.3;
- Craft and Structure RL.6-10.4, RL.6-10.5, RL.6-10.6;
- Integration of Knowledge and Ideas RL9-10.7.

ELA Reading: Informational Texts Standards
- Key Ideas and Details RI.6-10.1, RI.6-10.2, RI.6-10.3;
- Craft and Structure RI.6-10.4, RI.6-10.5, RI.6-10.6;
- Integration of Knowledge and Ideas RI.6-10.7, RI.6-10.8.

ELA Writing Standards
- Text Types and Purposes W.6-10.1, W.6-10.2, W.6-10.3;
- Production and Distribution of Writing W.6-10.4, W.6-10.5, W.6-10.6;
- Research to Build and Present Knowledge W.6-10.7, W.6-10.8, W.6-10.9.

ELA Writing Standards
- Comprehension and Collaboration SL.6-10.1, SL.6-10.2, SL.6-10.3;
- Presentation of Knowledge and Ideas SL.6-10.4, SL.6-10.5, SL.6-10.6.

A General Approach

It is highly recommended that you read Scott McCloud's *Understanding Comics*[1], specifically pages 60-63, which deal with closure; pages 70-72, which deal with panel transitions; and 152-155, which deal with word/picture combinations. Depending on the needs of your class, you can have students learn these specific terms and use them to identify the different transition and combination styles. Alternatively, you can utilize your understanding of them to guide discussion, when examining specific panels or pages.

Highlight individual panels and or pages, and ask the following questions:
- What is going on in this panel or on this page?
- What is the purpose of the specific pictures in telling the story? How do they enhance the words?
- Why did the creator choose to put these words and pictures together in this way?
- How does color affect the scene?
- What do we learn about the character from the images?
- What mood is being set and how?

Examine the specific sequence of panels:
- Why did the creator put these panels in this particular order?
- What's happening between the panels?
- How does the transition between these panels indicate things like mood and character?
- How do the panel transitions affect the speed of the scene?
- Why did the creator choose this speed?

LET'S GET ACTIVE!
A great exercise is to have students act out a short scene in the book, getting them to fill in the action occurring between the panels. This demonstrates to them that the gutter (that space between panels) is just as important as the other storytelling elements in the book.

---

1. *McCloud, Scott, 1960-. Understanding Comics: the Invisible Art. New York: HarperPerennial, 1994.*

Pre-Reading Activities

- What does the cover tell you about the story? Does it make you want to read the book? Why or why not?

- Edmonia Lewis lived from 1844 to 1907. What were the rights for women at that time? What were the rights for minorities?

- What was the Civil Rights movement?

- Look at page 3. What do you think you know about the character based on this first page? What sort of challenges do you think she faced in terms of "social class, wealth, language, and racial equality"?

Discussion Questions

Questions about specific pages:

1. Examine the panels on page 4. Why is each panel focused in this way? What are the key details being shown and why?

2. On page 5, who do you think Edmonia was scandalizing and why? Have you ever exaggerated a story for effect?

3. Based on page 6 panel 1, what do you believe Edmonia thinks about her new situation? How do you know?

4. Describe the panels on page 11 and how they are contributing to the story. How do the first and last panel enhance each other? How does the first panel compare to the first panel on page 13? What is the effect of this?

5. Why is page 14 a splash page? How does it affect the pace of the story and you as a reader?

6. How does the layout of panel 4 on page 21 reinforce the text?

7. On page 22, panel 2, do you think the two people standing in her workshop are statues, people who are there, or her imagination? What is the effect of this?

8. On page 26, what is the effect of the transition from panel 1 to panel 2?

9. Look at page 28 and discuss the layout. How does breaking out of the traditional panel layout change the storytelling? How does it establish or change the mood and pace?

10. What does Edmonia think about the criticism of her work, based on page 30, panel 3? How do you know?

11. Look at the bottom panel of page 33. Describe what is happening. What are the lightning bolts? Who is being depicted? What are the reactions of the various characters?

12. What are the viewers' reactions to the sculpture of *Cleopatra* on page 38? How can you tell? Why did they react that way? Why would J.S. Ingraham say that *Cleopatra* was "the most remarkable piece of sculpture in the American section"?

13. Why do you never see the two men's faces on page 43? How does this contribute to the story?

14. Describe the panels on page 52 and how they serve to help tell the story.

12.

General Questions:

1. What is an abolitionist? What role did they play in Edmonia's life?

2. What is the difference between the education for men, for women, and for "students of color" at Oberlin College (see page 7)? Why was it this way? Why were the groups perceived so differently?

3. What challenges did Edmonia face at Oberlin College and why? How did she overcome these challenges?

4. Why do you think Edmonia was accused of poisoning her two classmates?

5. What kind of workspace did Edmonia like to work in, according to the images in the book?

6. Why do you think it was important for so many women to interview Edmonia and write articles about her?

7. On page 24, Edmonia says, "Some praise me because I am a colored girl, and I don't want that kind of praise. I had rather you point out my defects, for that will teach me something." Why would she want to avoid praise and instead be criticized?

8. What sort of things did Edmonia do to change the conversation about the fact that she was a woman and Black? How did she stand up to people's prejudices?

9. On page 33, Edmonia has tea with some peers in the art world. What are the challenges they are facing? What do you think about these challenges? How do they compare to the challenges Edmonia faces? What do you believe Edmonia thinks about these challenges?

10. Do you find the structure of the story effective? Pages 42 to 49 are about events that occur much later. Does it work at this point in the story? Do you think it should have been included at another point in the book? Why or why not?

11. Why do you think Edmonia made so many busts of male figures?

12. Does Edmonia's story inspire you? Why or why not?

Post-Reading Activities

Reading:

1. Describe Edmonia by selecting 3 to 6 panels that reflect the different aspects of her personality.

2. Find 3 examples of using a black background in a panel. How does it change the story? What is the effect of the black background?

3. Go back to the question you answered during the pre-reading activities, based on page 3. Did your ideas about Edmonia and her challenges change after reading the whole book? What do you think now about the statement "She was a pioneer, an innovator, and an incredibly brave woman with a cheerful, bold personality"?

4. What do you believe the author wants you to think or feel about Edmonia Lewis? Find examples of panels and text which support your opinion.

Writing:

1. Edmonia Lewis encountered many people and had many experiences, good and bad, throughout her life. Write a newspaper article in which you interview Edmonia on an element of her life that interests you.

2. On page 34, Edmonia receives a letter from one of her supporters, Lydia Maria Child. Imagine what Edmonia would say to her in a reply. Write a letter to Lydia Maria Child as Edmonia Lewis.

3. Write a prose version of page 17, 26, or 52. What are some of the differences between prose and comic storytelling?

Speaking:

1. In groups, examine pictures of the artwork of Edmonia Lewis. What do you think about the pieces? How do they make you feel? Do you think they accomplish what Edmonia wanted them to accomplish?

2. Pick a piece of Edmonia's art (or have one assigned by your teacher) and present it to the class. Explain at what stage of her career she made it, and how it reflects her life at that time and as a whole.

3. "Edmonia was clear that she had no desire to be judged by her skin color before her art." (p.40) Stage a debate on the pros and cons of portraying her subjects more true to their appearances. Do these pros and cons change as time goes on, and we look back on her work?

Integrating:

1. Several women are mentioned in the book: Anne Whitney, Harriet Hosmer, Lydia Maria Child, Elizabeth Peabody, Anna Quincy Waterston, and Laura Bullard, to name a few. These women all worked in ways that went against 19th century gender norms. Research one of these women and write a comparison of the challenges faced by that person and Edmonia Lewis. What challenges did they share?

2. "*The Song of Hiawatha*, a poem by Henry Wadsworth Longfellow, was a common muse for Edmonia Lewis. Possibly because the poem was inspired by Ojibwe legends." (p.22) Read the poem. Why do you think this poem had an impact on Edmonia? How can you see its inspiration in her works?

3. Edmonia Lewis made sculptures of many people; among them, Robert Gould Shaw, Frederick Douglass, Henry Wadsworth Longfellow, and Charles Sumner. Research and write a biography on one of these figures and explain why you think Edmonia Lewis chose to sculpt him. What about him perhaps was inspiring to her?

1871 BUST OF
HENRY WADSWORTH
LONGFELLOW